DK Life Stories

Jesse OWENS

DK Life Stories

Jesse OWENS

by James Buckley Jr

Illustrated by Charlotte Ager

Penguin
Random
House

Senior Editors Marie Greenwood, Roohi Sehgal
Assistant Editor Seeta Parmar
Senior Art Editor Ann Cannings
Project Art Editor Roohi Rais
Art Editor Mohd Zishan
Assistant Art Editor Simran Lakhiani
Jacket Coordinator Issy Walsh
Jacket Designer Dheeraj Arora
DTP Designers Sachin Gupta, Nand Kishor Acharya
Project Picture Researcher Sakshi Saluja
Production Editor Dragana Puvacic
Production Controller John Casey
Managing Editors Jonathan Melmoth, Monica Saigal
Managing Art Editors Diane Peyton Jones, Ivy Sengupta
Delhi Team Head Malavika Talukder
Creative Director Helen Senior
Publishing Director Sarah Larter

Subject Consultant Jacqueline Edmondson
Literacy Consultant Stephanie Laird

First published in Great Britain in 2020
by Dorling Kindersley Limited
One Embassy Gardens, 8 Viaduct Gardens,
London, SW11 7BW

Published in Great Britain
by Dorling Kindersley Limited

A CIP catalogue record for this book
is available from the British Library.
ISBN: 978-0-2414-1384-5

Printed and bound in China

For the curious

www.dk.com

Dear Reader,

The story of American Olympic hero Jesse Owens is covered in gold for the four medals he won in 1936. It's also covered with racism, which he battled with throughout his life. Jesse grew up in the segregated South, but fought his way out using speed and courage. After defeating the insane ideas of Nazism, he returned to a United States that remained divided by race, even as it united in celebrating his victories.

Jesse's story mirrors the struggle of African Americans in the 20th century. It also tells the tale of how some star athletes struggled to reach the same heights away from their sports as they achieved in them. Jesse was one of the fastest people of all time, but he could not outrun all the troubles in his life.

But Jesse's is also a comeback story. After reaching the heights of fame and then falling, he climbed back to a place of love and respect – and that might have been the greatest victory of all.

Now, let's go back to a time when the world needed a hero. On your marks... get set... READ!

Happy reading,
James Buckley Jr

The life of...
Jesse **Owens**

Chapter 1

A slow start

Jesse Owens was born into extreme poverty in Oakville, Alabama, USA, in 1913. As soon as he could, Jesse started a lifelong race to escape it.

Jesse was born James Cleveland Owens, about 50 years after slavery officially ended in the United States. However, life for African Americans was still very difficult, especially in the Southern States. Jesse's parents – Henry and Emma Owens – were the children of people who had been enslaved. The end of the Civil War and the Emancipation Proclamation had set enslaved people free. However, being free and being safe and successful were different things.

What is the Emancipation Proclamation?

This was a document written in 1863 by President Abraham Lincoln that officially freed all people who were enslaved in the Southern United States.

Henry and Emma married in 1895. Henry worked as a sharecropper in the town of Oakville, Alabama. He worked long hours in the fields for very little money. Together they had 12 children – though three sadly died at birth. Of those surviving children, the three oldest were daughters, and the next six were sons. This large family lived in a small wooden house with just three rooms. When they were old enough, the children often joined Henry picking crops and tending the fields. The younger kids attended school in a one-room schoolhouse, when there was a teacher available, that is.

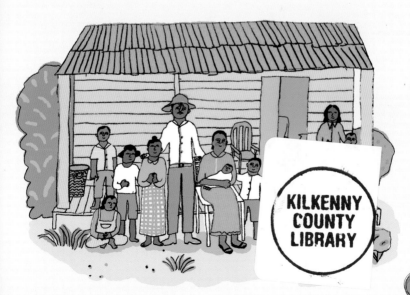

SHARECROPPING

This was a type of farming often found in the South in the years after the Civil War (1861–1865), which was fought between the Southern slave-owning states and the Northern states. African Americans who wanted to earn money farming generally could not afford to buy their own land. So they rented it, usually from white landowners. The farmers had to pay the rent with a share of the crops they grew. Unfortunately, the system worked in favour of the landowners. They gave the farmers seeds and gear in return for more crops. However, if the crops failed, the farmers fell into debt and often never earned a profit on their work. Some called it "slavery by another name".

Sharecroppers working in a cotton field in the Mississippi Delta, in the southeastern USA.

Throughout the Southern United States, tens of thousands of African Americans worked and lived like this. The white governments of those

Segregated water fountains in the "Jim Crow" era.

states passed "Jim Crow" laws that created a two-part way of life. For example, black people could not go to theatres with white people, or share most public toilets or pools. African-American children were educated at separate schools. In some places there were even separate drinking fountains!

In 1913, while living this hard life, the Owens family got what Emma called a "gift child". James Cleveland (Jesse), her seventh son, was born on 12 September of that year. Everyone called him J.C. Early in his life, J.C. struggled.

What were the "Jim Crow" laws? Rules that created separate public places for white people and black people.

One of the problems of living in poverty is that it is hard to get the right nutrients you need to stay healthy. Meat was a treat in the Owens house, typically only served on public holidays. Beans were the usual family meal, along with a few vegetables from their farm. Plus, the house had no heating and no electricity.

J.C. was a small baby and a small child. As a result of the family's poor living conditions, he was often very ill. He had fevers. He caught bad colds. Several times he had painful boils. Emma had to carve them out with a hot knife before they got infected.

Despite this, J.C. had fond memories of his hard young life. "We used to have a lot of fun," he said later. "We always ate. The fact that we didn't have steak? Who had steak?" Not all of his memories were good ones, though. He told an interviewer once that "there was often no money to buy clothing. I sometimes didn't have enough to cover myself." Jesse remembered one time that he had been embarrassed by being seen by girls when he was wearing barely any clothes.

DID YOU KNOW?

Jesse's family regularly attended the Oakville Baptist Church near their home.

But young J.C. got stronger as he grew up. He loved playing games with the many children in his neighbourhood. Most were the sons and daughters of sharecroppers. They all lived in poverty, but this did not stop them enjoying themselves and having fun.

Even at this early age, games that included lots of running were J.C.'s favourites.

Life remained hard, however. Then, in 1915, it got harder still – thanks to an insect. The boll weevil arrived in the South and destroyed millions of dollars worth of crops, mostly cotton. Many farms failed, and thousands of people lost jobs and money.

Amid all this, people like the Owens family looked for a way out. One of J.C.'s sisters, Lillie, moved north to the big city of Cleveland, Ohio, looking for work. She was so thrilled with what she found there that she encouraged her parents to join her.

Lillie's father, Henry, went first, with two of her brothers. He soon had a well-paid job and he wrote to Emma back at the tiny wooden house. Soon, the whole Owens family was on the move to a better life.

"I always loved running. I wasn't very good at it, but I loved it because **it was something** you could do **all by yourself.** You could go in any direction, **fast** or **slow** as you wanted."

Jesse Owens, in his book *Jesse: A Spiritual Autobiography*, 1978

2

Picking up speed

In about 1922 (no one is sure of the exact year), J.C.'s mother, Emma, got word from his father up in Cleveland.

Emma sold everything the family owned for only $24 (that's the same as about $800 today). After a long train ride, the family were together again, this time in a house with room enough for all. The Owens family were not alone in moving north. Throughout the 1920s and 1930s, several million African Americans moved from the South to large cities in the North. They moved from farms to find jobs in factories. This movement came to be called "The Great Migration".

USA

Cleveland

Oakville

The African-American families still faced discrimination, or unjust treatment, due to the colour of their skin, but it was usually not as bad as their experiences in the South. Most earned enough money to rent good apartments or houses.

THE GREAT MIGRATION

In the years after World War I (1914–1918), almost 2 million African Americans moved from farms in the South to cities in the North, in search of a better life. By the time of World War II (1939–1945), northern cities such as Chicago, Cleveland, Detroit, and New York had large African-American populations.

Others were able to start their own businesses. In their new home town, J.C. and his siblings went straight to work part-time. J.C. worked at a shoe shop, polishing boots and sweeping floors. And for the first time in their lives, the Owens children went to a normal school, with different year groups and classrooms. At Bolton Elementary, in Cleveland, J.C. got a new nickname. J.C.'s teacher did not understand his Southern accent, and thought he said his name was "Jesse". The young boy was too shy to correct her, so he became Jesse Owens for the rest of his life.

Along with a new name, Jesse had a new experience – going to school with white children. Most of the kids in the Owens family's neighbourhood had also come from other places. The white pupils were the children of parents who had come from Southern and Eastern Europe. Jesse found that he could make friends easily with kids from all over.

After Bolton, Jesse went to Fairmount Junior High, starting in seventh grade. He was 14 years old. There he met a girl called Ruth Solomon. They soon became close and started dating. Jesse spent his breaktimes racing around the playground, showing off his favourite thing – running. He was watched

by a man named Charles Riley, a teacher at the school and the track coach. Riley saw something special in how Jesse ran. He encouraged Jesse to become more serious about racing and join the school's track team. Very quickly, Riley was proved right – Jesse really was something special. When he was in eighth grade, he ran 100 yards in 11 seconds – just 1.6 seconds slower than the world record at the time! At a school track meet, Jesse leaped 6.98 m (22 ft 11¾ in) in the long jump. That set a national junior high record.

Riley helped Jesse improve year after year. He also gave his young star a new goal. In 1928, Riley arranged for the great Charles Paddock to talk to his athletes, and especially to Jesse. The American sprinter Paddock was known as "the world's fastest human". He had won the 1920 Olympic gold medal in the 100 metres, and earned a silver in 1924.

CHARLES PADDOCK

A World War I veteran, Charles Paddock was the first to be called "the fastest man alive". Paddock was famous for his leaping finishes as he almost jumped across the line.

At one point, Paddock had also held the world record for the 100 metres, at 10.4 seconds. Jesse was dazzled to meet such a big star. Paddock represented something new – now Jesse wanted to be like Paddock… a champion. Together, he and Riley set out to make it happen.

As their time together went on, Riley treated Jesse like one of his sons. For his part, Jesse remembered that "Coach Riley taught me how to behave. His influence on me kept us out of trouble." Jesse went on to say that Riley had proved to him that a white man can understand and love a black man.

Riley's support proved to be hugely important. In 1929, Jesse's father was badly injured in a car accident. He could not work for a long time. His older children had to leave school to help the family. In addition, the Great Depression started later that year and millions of people lost their jobs. Jesse, however, stayed at school. He knew his education was important if he wanted to move up in the world.

THE GREAT DEPRESSION

On 29 October 1929, the New York Stock Exchange suddenly lost value. Companies had to close and millions of people lost their life savings. Unemployment and poverty skyrocketed in the USA. The Great Depression, as it came to be known, lasted until the mid-1930s.

Jesse with his coach, Charles Riley.

In 1930, Jesse moved up to attend East Technical High School. Riley came along as an assistant coach for the track team. That summer, under Riley's guidance, Jesse even did a trial for the US Olympic team. Although he ran well, Jesse was still learning, and did not make the final qualifying events. The Olympics would have to wait.

Chapter 3

College man

Jesse headed into his senior year of high school determined to do even better on the track.

However, he had another reason to succeed. Remember Ruth Solomon? She and Jesse had been dating for several years. On 8 August 1932, Ruth gave birth to a daughter named Gloria. At the age of 18, Jesse was now a dad.

He still had to finish school, however. Ruth remained with her parents, and they helped care for Gloria while Ruth went to school herself. Jesse just kept running – and winning. By the time his high-school track career was over, he had won 75 of the 79 events he entered! With Riley's guidance, Jesse had created a running style that worked perfectly for his skills. He remained almost upright, keeping his shoulders back. His stride was loose and easy, even as he increased his speed as he ran.

Jesse's success on the track had made him a popular boy at school, and he was elected president of the student council. The track team chose him as its captain, too. In May 1933, he won three events at a big meet in Chicago. A month later, he hit the headlines for his feats at the

DID YOU KNOW?

Several student council presidents have gone on to become famous politicians, such as Hillary Clinton.

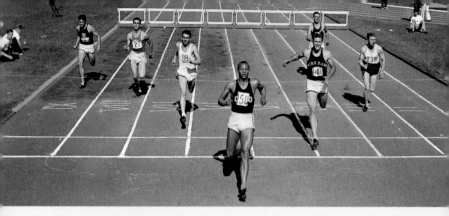

Jesse won the 220-yard low hurdles race, even though he rarely practised it.

National Interscholastic Track and Field Championships. East Tech scored 54 points and won the team title. Jesse was responsible for 30 of those all by himself. He had almost as many solo points as the entire second-place team! Cleveland welcomed him and his team home with a parade that ended at City Hall.

TRACK AND FIELD

Track and field is divided into two main groups – track events, such as running and hurdles, and field events, such as throwing and jumping. Below are the main types of track-and-field events practised today.

1. Long distance
2. Middle distance
3. Sprint
4. Relay
5. Hurdles

1. Long jump
2. High jump
3. Javelin
4. Shot put

5. Pole vault
6. Hammer
7. Discus

Thanks to Jesse's skill on the track, colleges around the country wanted him. No one in Jesse's family had ever gone to college, so this was a huge deal. He considered the University of Michigan and Indiana University, among others. In the end, he chose Ohio State University (OSU), but his choice was controversial. At the time, OSU was considered by many African Americans to be racist and biased against them. Newspapers aimed at African-American audiences demanded that Jesse choose another college. "Many and long were the outcries against his decision," wrote the *Call and Post* in Cleveland.

Ohio State University (OSU) was founded in 1870.

Slavery was long gone in America, but racism continued in many ways. Though he arrived as a star athlete, Jesse got few privileges at OSU. He had to live in a separate building for African-American students, as well as eat in a separate dining hall. When the team travelled, especially to Southern colleges, Jesse and the other African-American athletes could not go to the same restaurants as their white teammates, or shower at the same gyms.

Also, for all athletes, there were no scholarships for track in those days, so Jesse had to find work to pay for books, food, and college. He worked for a time as a lift operator in a state office building. He was later a waiter and worked at a petrol station.

Jesse had to work to pay for college.

In class, Jesse struggled. He had spent most of high school working and running, and his grades were never that good. For a while, as a freshman (first-year student) at OSU, he was on academic probation – that is, he could not compete until he achieved higher grades. He worked hard and got off probation in time to set new Big Ten Conference records for freshmen in the 100-yard and 220-yard dashes. Jesse enjoyed working with a new coach, Larry Snyder. Like Riley, Snyder became a kind of

Larry Snyder spent many hours coaching Jesse.

father figure for Jesse, and a white man that he felt he could trust. "Coach Snyder proved to me that prejudice is a matter of choice, not colouring," Jesse said years later.

After a summer at home with his parents, Ruth, and his daughter, Gloria, Jesse returned to Ohio State in the autumn of 1934. He was just a few months away from becoming a legend.

An **amazing** afternoon

After dominating in the indoor track season in early 1935, Jesse was set to lead the OSU team into the Big Ten finals.

But a few days before the big event, to be held in Ann Arbor, Michigan, disaster struck. Jesse was coming down some steps in the house he shared with other OSU athletes. He slipped and bounced on his back to the bottom. He spent several days in bed. Then he tried soaking in a hot bath to loosen the muscles. Even to get to Michigan, his friends had to help him walk to the car. The night before the event, the OSU trainers tried rubdowns and heating pads. Coach Snyder was not at all

THE BIG TEN

In 1896, a group of seven Midwestern colleges formed the Western Intercollegiate Conference. They organized athletic events among their college teams. By 1917, after three more colleges had joined, they were called the Big Ten. Today – oddly – there are 14 teams in the Big Ten!

sure his star would be ready for the team's biggest day.

On the day of the big meet, Jesse woke up sore, but no longer in great pain. It was a warm, sunny day and after he had loosened up at the track, he felt as though he could give his events a shot. It proved to be the right decision.

The 100-yard dash came first at 3:15 pm Jesse dug into the small divots (holes) he and the other runners had carved in the dirt track. This helped them push off at the start. At the starter's signal, the racers burst down the track. Head up, gliding as always, Jesse whizzed past the finish line in first place. The official timers' watches

showed his time as 9.31 to 9.34 seconds.
By the rules of the day, this was
rounded up to an official time
of 9.4 seconds. Jesse had
matched the world record!

Ten minutes later, he stood
at the end of the long-jump
runway. He asked a teammate
to put a handkerchief at 7.9 m
(26 ft) as a target. Jesse gathered
himself, took off, and sprinted. At top speed,
he leaped… and landed 8.13 m (26 ft 8¼ in)
away. It was another world record, beating the
old mark by more than 15 centimetres!

However, Jesse had not finished.

At 3:34, he began the 220-yard race.
Most 220-yard, or 200-metre events today,
are run around the curve of the track, but
at this meet, the race was run in a straight line.
Jesse's amazing day continued when
he set a second world record, with
a time of 20.3 seconds. No one
had ever set two new world records

in one day; Jesse had just done it in about half an hour!

After resting for about 20 minutes, it was time to hit the track again. This time, Jesse was running the 220-yard low hurdles. It was not his best event, but that didn't matter. When the times were recorded, he had done it again. His time of 22.6 seconds was the fourth world record he had set or tied in less than an hour! *Sports Illustrated* magazine later called Jesse's

Jesse clearing the last hurdle in the 220-yard hurdle race.

Olympic sprinter Eddie Tolan congratulating Jesse as fellow athlete Willis Ward looks on.

feat the "greatest single-day performance in athletic history".

However, Jesse and OSU still had work to do. As they had won the Big Ten, the team had earned a spot in the National Collegiate Athletic Association (NCAA) National Championships. OSU stopped first in Los Angeles to race against the University of California, Los Angeles (UCLA). Even though by this time Jesse was a national hero, he was still an African American. While the OSU team stayed in a hotel, Jesse and his teammate Mel Walker were forced to find other lodgings. They ended up staying at a fraternity house at the University of Southern California (USC).

what is a fraternity house?

Fraternities are groups of students. A group may live together in a fraternity house.

Still, Jesse managed to find time to have fun. While the team stayed in Los Angeles for its meet against USC, he met a young woman named Quincella Nickerson. For the next few days, they were seen out and about together, often in her bright blue car. Since Jesse was now famous, he was often photographed with Quincella. Those photos ran in newspapers, and those newspapers included some in Cleveland. Ruth was not pleased.

Back in California, Jesse and OSU headed to Berkeley for the national college championships. Once again, Jesse won all four of his events. OSU scored 40.2 points; Jesse earned 40 of them. His personal total was more than that of all but one other team that day!

After competing at a national Amateur Athletic Union (AAU) event in Nebraska on the way home, Jesse arrived in Cleveland in July 1935. He and Ruth were married the next day. She was not going to let him wriggle out of his responsibilities, no matter how famous he was!

Reverend Ernest Hall marrying Ruth and Jesse at Ruth's house.

39

5

Should I stay or go?

**After his feats at the Big Ten meet, Jesse
was clearly the top track-and-field athlete
in the world.**

The place where the world's best show their
stuff is the Summer Olympics, held every four
years. In 1936, the Olympics would take place in
Berlin, Germany. That was not the only reason
Germany was in the news. In recent years,
the country had undergone a huge change.
Adolf Hitler and his Nazi Party had taken
over the government. They spread racist and
anti-Jewish policies, and were clearly heading
towards war... and worse.

By the autumn of 1935, there was a lot of
talk about the United States boycotting – or
refusing to attend – the Olympics in protest
against Nazi actions and beliefs. Many Americans

believed, rightly, that Nazi policies were harming Jewish people and other minorities. However, a few Americans thought that the stories coming out of Germany were exaggerated.

African-American newspapers and leaders were among the loudest voices, partly because

NAZI GERMANY

In 1933, Adolf Hitler took over as Chancellor of Germany. He was the leader of the National Socialist Party, or the Nazi Party. Nazi policies were racist and anti-Semitic (prejudiced against Jewish people). They said that only "pure" Germans deserved to live. Hitler spewed hate and raised a huge army that in 1939 started World War II. Hitler and the Nazis were defeated at the end of the war, in 1945.

Hitler and the Nazis considered people of African descent to be lesser humans than European "German Aryans". Jesse was once again torn, as he had been with his decision about college. He just wanted to run. He didn't want to be involved with politics, and yet he did think that if there was discrimination, they should withdraw. However, Coach Snyder convinced him to stay out of the argument. "There won't be a boycott," Snyder told him.

The debate raged in the papers for months. At one point, US Olympic leader Avery Brundage flew to Germany to see what was happening.

AVERY BRUNDAGE

As the leader of the Amateur Athletic Union (AAU), Avery ran American amateur sport for almost 30 years. He later became the president of the International Olympic Committee, the only American ever to hold the job. Avery battled to preserve amateur rules even as sport changed around him.

"If there is discrimination against minorities in Germany then we must withdraw from the Olympics."

Jesse Owens,
1935

43

DID YOU KNOW?

The 1916 Summer Olympics were due to take place in Berlin, but were cancelled because of World War I.

To the surprise of many, Avery returned to say that Jewish people in Germany were being treated well and that he was perfectly comfortable with the idea of holding the Games in Germany. In reality, he had only seen what the government wanted him to see, and Jewish people were facing growing discrimination.

THE OLYMPIC GAMES

The modern Olympic Games are sporting events that take place every four years, with the Summer and Winter Games being held at two-year intervals. Athletes from more than 200 countries come together to compete in sports including swimming, gymnastics, tennis, and, of course, track and field. New events are always being added, such as surfing and skateboarding. In Jesse's day, all Olympic athletes had to be amateurs. That is, they could not be paid for their work in sport. Today, the amateurs-only rule in the Olympics no longer applies.

Eventually, Avery got his way. The AAU, which ran track in the United States, voted to send a track team to the Olympics.

Meanwhile, in early 1936, Jesse had a problem closer to home. He had failed a psychology class, so he was not allowed to be on the track team in the winter. As he worked to improve his grades, he found a way to use his fame to help others. Along with Larry Snyder, Jesse travelled to poor schools in rural West Virginia. He spoke to students there as part of a health programme aimed at young African Americans. Jesse hoped his example of hard work and a focus on staying fit would inspire the students.

When Jesse passed the class and returned to the team, he kept winning. In the spring of

1936, he won four national championships again. He also won six titles in AAU events.

To no one's surprise, Jesse easily won the 100-metre, 200-metre, and long-jump events at the US Olympic Qualifying meet in New York City. Next stop: Berlin.

Though some aeroplanes were making trips across the Atlantic Ocean, for a group this big, the only way to go was by ship. The American Olympic team, plus coaches, trainers, and organizers, piled onto the SS *Manhattan* in New York Harbor. Thousands of people crowded on the pier to see them off on their nine-day trip.

Athletes being athletes, they didn't enjoy the slow pace of the ship. The wide wooden decks and walkways were turned into practice places. Jesse and other runners jogged around the massive ship. Other athletes stretched or worked

Jesse training on deck with Olympic teammates Ralph Metcalfe (centre) and Frank C. Wykoff (right).

out with weights. Some, however, did not do as well. Food on the fancy ship was everywhere… and it was good! Some athletes were not used to it and gained so much weight during the trip that they did not perform well in Germany.

For his part, Jesse did not overeat. He stayed active and ate well. On the last night of the trip, he was voted the "best dressed" among the athletes. Jesse thought that was odd, since all he owned was the single suit he had come aboard wearing!

Chapter 6

Welcome to **Berlin**!

Jesse arrived in Germany to a warm welcome. He was eager to start pursuing Olympic glory.

Even though official German government policy discriminated against black people, the German people were thrilled to see Jesse. His world records had made him a hero to sports lovers everywhere. He was mobbed for autographs as he and the rest of the US team made their way from the dock to their hotel. He was woken up in his hotel room by people banging on the windows to take his picture. German people chanted his name whenever he appeared: "*Jezz-EE, Jezz-EE!*"

Meanwhile, German officials made sure that their country did not reflect what was really happening. Anti-Jewish signs and banners were taken down. Streets were swept clean and the destruction of Jewish neighbourhoods was covered up. Soldiers in the SS – the hated secret police – did not wear their black uniforms. One reporter wrote, "The effect will surely be to send thousands of foreigners home with excellent opinions of the effects of dictatorship." Basically, Nazi Germany was going to use the Games to prove that its policies were correct. Jesse and others were about to help prove them wrong.

The Olympic opening ceremonies were held on 1 August 1936. Jesse was not in the stadium. Since he and several other sprinters had races

later that day or the next morning, they
rested back at the Olympic Athletes' Village.
They watched some of the ceremony on
a fairly new invention – TV. "It's like radio
with pictures," Jesse told Coach Snyder. As
usual, the American flag was not lowered
(called "dipping") as it passed the German
leader. All the other flags did and many
countries also gave Hitler the stiff-armed
salute he used in Germany. The Americans
did not.

**what does
dipping the
flag mean?**

Traditionally, national flags are lowered when
passing the local national leader. American flags
are never dipped, a tradition dating back to 1908.

THE 1936 OLYMPIC GAMES

The Nazis were a tiny part of German politics in 1931 when the International Olympic Committee awarded the 1936 Games to Berlin. By the time the Games started, worldwide opinion had turned against Germany, but the Games went on. Nearly 4,000 athletes from 49 countries took part. Germany used the Olympics to promote its national goals.

The Berlin Olympics were the first to feature the now-famous Olympic torch relay from Athens to the site of the Games.

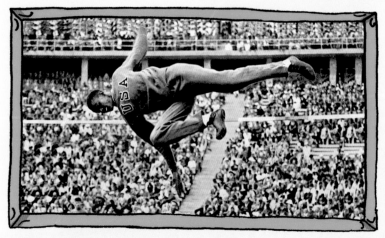
Cornelius warming up before his high jump.

Later on that Saturday, an African American named Cornelius Johnson won the high-jump competition. He also helped start an Olympic myth that is still discussed today. To that point in the day's events, Hitler had invited all the gold medal winners to his box to congratulate them. The first had been Germans; the next, a group of athletes from Finland. But about 10 minutes before Johnson won his event, Hitler left the stadium. Reporters disagreed about whether or not the German leader left because he did not want to meet a black athlete.

The next morning, Jesse's Olympic Games began. He had to run in two qualifying races for the 100 metres. Naturally, he won them both. In the second, he set a new world record at 10.3 seconds; the next day, the record was disallowed when officials said the wind at his back was too strong. Jesse just shrugged when he heard the news.

On Monday 3 August, Jesse easily won the semifinal of the 100 metres. That put him into the finals of the most famous sprint race in the world. Watching from the stands again was Hitler.

In the final, Jesse roared to victory, tying the world record at 10.3 seconds. He was an Olympic champion! "This is the happiest day in my life," he said after the race.

After Jesse's victory in the 100-metre final, press photographers swarmed to capture his moment of triumph.

54

Jesse stood to attention as the US national anthem rang out in Berlin's Olympic Stadium. And here's where the myth comes in. Since leaving the stadium on Sunday, Hitler had not met any other gold medalists. He had been accused of snubbing Johnson and apparently had decided not to risk any more criticism… so he didn't meet anyone – white, black, or otherwise. However, Jesse did claim that Hitler waved down at him when the gold medalist walked in front of the leader's box in the stands.

That was not enough for most people, however. Newspapers were angry at what they saw as Hitler's snub of Jesse.

At the time, Jesse was not bothered by Hitler's reaction to him. Sadly, as an African American, being turned away because of the colour of his skin was something Jesse was all too familiar with at home, to say nothing of Nazi Germany.

Jesse wore a traditional
laurel wreath on his
head after winning gold.

A **magical** moment

On Tuesday, 4 August, Jesse had a very busy day – and helped create a great Olympic memory.

First, he ran in qualifying heats of the 200-metre race, setting an Olympic record at 21.1 seconds. Next up was qualifying for the long jump. Jesse had to jump 7.13 m (23 ft 5 in) to make the next rounds. He had jumped that far at school! He took a quick warm-up run. The official raised his red flag for an illegal jump. What Jesse didn't know was that the American style of a practice jump was NOT part of the Olympics. The foul meant that he had just two more tries to make the jump. Nervous, he fell short on his second jump. This was looking bad. If he fouled or did not jump far enough, he would be out of the event.

Then something remarkable happened. With a surprise bit of sportsmanship, a German athlete changed the course of Jesse's Olympics... and perhaps his life.

The star athlete of the whole games, Luz Long, approached Jesse. Luz was a long-jump champion, though he had not jumped as far as Jesse's record from the year before. And he was the enemy – not only a competitor, but a German.

LUZ LONG

While studying to be a lawyer in Germany, Luz also became the best long jumper in Europe. He entered the Olympic Games as a firm favourite. In befriending Jesse, he angered Nazi officials. Sadly, Luz was killed fighting for the German army in 1943.

Luz with Jesse

Luz said, "You should draw a line far behind the take-off board. That way you'll be sure not to foul. You can make this jump with your eyes closed." Long jumpers have to jump from behind a wooden board on the runway. If they touch it at all, the jump does not count.

Jesse was shocked. Having his rival help him win was unexpected.

Jesse did what Luz had suggested and easily made the jump. The two men shook hands. It was such a simple thing. But this one moment between Jesse and Luz is now part of Olympic history. It highlights how athletes should care for each other and the sport – and that politics should stop at the edge of the track.

Later that afternoon, after Jesse had won another 200-metre qualifying race, Luz and Jesse competed again. In the semifinals, Jesse set a new Olympic record – again! – by jumping 7.87 m (25 ft 10 in). Luz's mark of 7.84 m (25 ft 8¾ in) also beat the old record.

At 5:45 pm, the two faced off with four other jumpers in the long-jump final. Jesse would not have been there if Luz had not helped him.

---

what is a qualifying race? To narrow the field for the finals, qualifying races are held. Only winners and high finishers advance to the next stage.

Luz went first and reached 7.87 m (25 ft 10 in), tying Jesse's record. The German fans went wild, hoping their champion could beat the great American. Jesse was happy that Luz had helped him, but he also knew that he would need his best to beat him. With a leap of 7.92 m (26 ft), breaking his own record, Jesse quieted the German fans.

Luz had one more chance. But as he took off, his foot hit the take-off board. It was a foul jump. The competition was over, and Jesse had won another gold medal. To cap things off, he took one more jump and soared further than any Olympian ever – 8.07 m (26 ft 5 ½ in).

The first person to congratulate Jesse was Luz Long. He raised Jesse's hand to the crowd. For years, Jesse remembered being amazed at Luz's actions. Here was his biggest rival – in a country that considered him a "non-human" – treating him like a friend and an equal.

That night, Jesse visited Luz at the Olympic Village to say *danke* (DAHN-keh), meaning "thank you". They talked and became friends. Reporters often saw them together during the remainder of the Olympic Games. Jesse considered what Luz had done as one of the most important moments in his life. "He was my strongest rival, yet it was he who advised me to adjust my run-up in the qualifying round and thereby helped me to win," Jesse said later in life.

Chapter 8

Running to **glory**

Jesse earned two more gold medals, but found himself in the middle of another politics-meets-sports controversy.

Another day, another gold medal. Jesse won the 200-meter semifinal easily and headed into the final as the huge favourite. The track was muddy after a day of rain, and the temperature was only about 12°C (55°F) – very cool for sprinters who do best in warm weather.

Mack Robinson

Jesse got off to another good start and flew around the curve of the track. He was far ahead of Mack Robinson in second place (Mack's brother, Jackie, would later become a pretty famous sportsman himself). When Jesse broke the finish-line tape, he ran right into history. He was the first person since 1900 to win three gold medals in one Olympic Games.

And that, most people thought, was that. Jesse was not scheduled to run in any more races. He had done everything he was supposed to do. The American coaches, however, had other plans. In those days, only four runners could take part in sprint relay races. Today, a country can use different runners in early heats of a relay and they all earn medals. In 1936, US coaches had chosen four men to run the 4x100-metre relay. Jesse was not among them… at first.

Jackie Robinson

What is a relay? A track event in which a series of athletes take turns passing a baton to each other for each leg of the race.

US coach Lawson Robertson announced that Marty Glickman, Sam Stoller, and Frank Wykoff had places. The fourth would be either Foy Draper or Ralph Metcalfe.

However, after they saw what Jesse had done and how popular he was, they pulled out Stoller and put Jesse in his place. They also swapped out Glickman for Draper and gave the fourth spot to Metcalfe, who had also won a medal. Sam Stoller and Marty Glickman were America's only Jewish Olympic track athletes that year.

To some, this was another instance of anti-Jewish, or anti-Semitic, beliefs. Glickman said at the time, and for many years afterwards, that he and Stoller were taken out to avoid embarrassing their Nazi hosts. Did Avery Brundage talk to the coaches? He disliked Jewish people almost as much as the Nazis did. For their part, the coaches said they had other reasons, including wanting to put their very fastest athletes in the race.

People's memories of the coaches' decision vary. Glickman said that Jesse stood up and said "I've got my medals, let Sam run." Others, including Stoller, thought that assistant coach Dean Cromwell wanted to make sure his USC athletes, Wykoff and Draper, got the spots.

However it happened, the result was no surprise. In front of the biggest crowd of the Games, more than 120,000 people, Jesse went first in the final and flew to the front. He passed the baton to Metcalfe, who increased the American lead. Draper carried on, and then handed to Wykoff on the anchor leg. The Americans' final time was 39.8 seconds, a new world record.

Coach Snyder met Jesse on the track and the two hugged while Snyder cried tears of joy for his athlete.

After less than a week of amazing performances, Jesse's Olympics were finally over. But he had not finished running. Only a day later, he and most of the American track team flew to Cologne, Germany, to run in an exhibition meet. They ran again in Hamburg and then flew to London, UK. Jesse had not planned for these extra events and he barely had time to pack for the trip. The AAU had arranged the events to make money, of which the athletes, of course, got none.

Jesse's gold-medal-winning leap in the long jump.

Jesse leaning into the finishing tape to win the 100-metre race.

esse burst around the turn before racing to a win in the 200 metres.

Jesse went first in the relay, leading the team to victory.

Why just three medals? Jesse gave one of them to a friend, Bojangles Robinson.

Jesse was tired after all the travel and all the running and jumping. Moreover, he was being offered huge sums of money to return to the US. His four gold medals had made him one of the most famous people in the world. Celebrities and theatres wanted to pay him to appear on stage. For a man who grew up poor in Alabama, this was more money than he ever thought he could earn. To accept it, of course, meant that he could not run for Ohio State or the US any more.

In the end, the decision was made for him. Coach Snyder and Jesse told the AAU that they were going home from London. They would not make another trip that the AAU had set up to Sweden.

Brundage and other American officials were angry… and greedy. Without Jesse, they

would not make nearly as much money.
So Brundage suspended Jesse from all AAU
events. It was a sudden end to one of the
greatest athletic careers in sports history.

From that moment on, Jesse Owens only
had one real job – being the famous Jesse
Owens. He would find that doing this job was
much harder than any race he had ever run.

An **un-welcome** home

**Once he returned home, Jesse found that
the colour of his skin mattered more
than the colour of the medals he had won.**

Jesse and Coach Snyder took the famous *Queen
Mary* cruise ship back from Europe to America.
The ship must have known who she had aboard.
The *Queen Mary* set a new speed record, crossing
the Atlantic in four days
and seven hours.

On the way
across, Jesse had time
to read the dozens of
telegrams and notes he
had received from people back in the United
States. Many were offers of money in exchange
for his appearance or use of his name. Jesse
thought he had it made, and that his family's

long-term money problems were over. Back in the States, American newspapers generally supported his decision to turn pro and get paid. Some African-American newspapers were a bit more suspicious. They wanted to see the deals completed, not just offered.

When the ship arrived in New York Harbor, Jesse was surprised to be greeted by his wife and his parents. They had travelled from Cleveland to meet his ship.

Jesse's mum (*left*) and wife were among the many people who welcomed home the Olympic hero.

Sadly, he would also discover that they had been turned away from most of the nice hotels in New York City. They only got a room with the help of a visiting Cleveland politician. In America, it didn't matter how famous your son was if your skin was black.

Among the people Jesse met upon his return was the African-American entertainer Bill "Bojangles" Robinson. A singer, dancer, and actor, Robinson wanted to help Jesse make money; although, of course, Robinson would be making money, too. He made more promises to Jesse before the Owens family headed back to Cleveland.

BILL "BOJANGLES" ROBINSON

Born in 1878, Bill Robinson was dancing for a living by the age of five. He went on to have a long career on stage as a tap dancer, singer, and entertainer. He later starred in films as well. His birthday, 25 May, is National Tap Dance Day.

Jese rode in an open-top car in a victory parade through the streets of New York City.

The welcome home was mighty indeed. A 24-km (15-mile) long parade through the city ended with a huge ceremony in Jesse's honour. Politicians and city leaders spoke. Jesse was awarded a gold watch. A few days later, he got a similar reception in Columbus, the Ohio state capital. Everyone from the governor down was there to welcome Jesse and Ruth. They even gave Jesse's wife a new set of fancy silverware. In early September, Jesse officially signed up with Robinson to be in the entertainer's shows. He also took part in another parade, this time for the whole US Olympic team. It took place in New York City, following a long tradition of "ticker tape" parades through the concrete canyons of Manhattan. This parade also headed north to Harlem, home to the city's African-American community. The people there were quick to notice that Jesse and other black athletes were all stuck together in a couple of cars near the back of the parade. Some watchers chanted that Jesse was being "Jim Crowed" even as he was being celebrated.

US President Franklin D. Roosevelt had never congratulated Jesse or invited him to the White House, as is traditional for successful athletes. As the black newspapers had suspected, many of the high-paying jobs did not come through. Robinson's agent

Franklin D. Roosevelt

TICKER TAPE PARADES

Beginning in 1886, parades through lower Manhattan became a way to honour famous people. From the windows above the parade route, workers would toss long, thin strips of paper that came from machines called "tickers" that reported the prices of stocks. The blizzard of paper flying over the honourees became a tradition. More than 200 such parades have been held for sports stars, military heroes, astronauts, visiting heads of state, and just about anyone else that New York City thinks deserves it.

did get Jesse some work appearing at banquets and such.

Jesse was making some money. He bought his parents a new house in Cleveland, including furniture, and Ruth got all the new clothes that she wanted. Overall, Jesse was less upset about the many broken promises than other people were. He tended to take things as they came instead of stewing over them.

Robinson's agent continued to drum up ways for Jesse to make money. One was controversial. Jesse flew to Havana, Cuba, for a special race. He would receive $2,000, more than most Americans would make in a year. Jesse's opponent? A horse.

At the time, Jesse did not express any problems with the idea. Other runners had

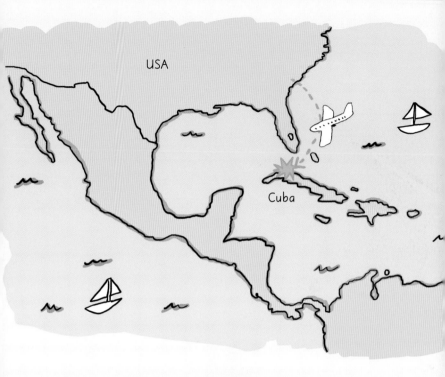

done the same. He told reporters he was "glad to get out on the track" again. However, in telling the story years later, he put it in a different light. He said he had felt humiliated to have had to race a horse for money. Probably, he realized how bad it looked in light of later racial struggles. At the time, it was not a big deal, but it became one later.

In late 1936, Jesse was named "Athlete of the Year" by the Associated Press – an easy choice!

The award capped off a whirlwind time after the Olympics that had held great promise. However, many of those promises did not come true. Jesse's next years would not be very golden.

"People say it was **degrading** for an Olympic champion to run **against a horse,** but what was I supposed to do? I had **four gold medals,** but you **can't eat** four gold medals."

Jesse Owens,
1971

Chapter 10

A **long,** tough **slog**

**At first, Jesse kept making money – lots
of it. But this was not to last...**

There is no doubt that Jesse's fame helped
him make money. He was hired to introduce
songs played at a big band concert. He helped
sponsor a black basketball team. He
worked for a time with a group helping
to create an African-American baseball

team in the Negro Leagues (the all-black professional leagues created because Major League Baseball did not allow black players). He gave speeches and appeared at banquets.

THE NEGRO LEAGUES

As a result of the ban on African Americans in Major League Baseball (MLB), African-American players organized their own professional teams. The Negro Leagues operated from the early 1900s until the mid-1950s. Thousands of great athletes were able to get paid to play baseball in front of cheering crowds. The Baseball Hall of Fame recognizes the best of these players, who missed out on the even greater fame provided by MLB.

The Chicago American Giants, owned by Rube Foster (*top centre*) played from 1911 to 1950.

Jesse operating a clothing press.

By 1938, Jesse had made quite a bit of money. Unfortunately, he had spent nearly all of it. To try to make more, he did a business deal, but it didn't work out. Jesse had teamed up with a pair of white businessmen to open a chain of laundries. The Jesse Owens Dry Cleaning Company offered a "speedy" service (get it?). A dozen stores opened in Ohio and Jesse made enough money to buy a new house. Then his partners vanished. It turned out they had cheated Jesse and left him responsible for all of the company's debts.

Then, Jesse had to pay taxes on money he had earned after the Olympics. Eventually, he declared bankruptcy, which means admitting to a court that you don't have enough money to pay your bills. It was humiliating, but Jesse just kept running.

One reason Jesse had to keep working and making money was that his family was growing. Ruth gave birth to a second daughter, named Marlene, in 1939. Another daughter, Beverly, came along in 1940. In the same year, Jesse went back to study at Ohio State, working part-time as a coach. He thought a college degree would help open other doors for him. He found studying difficult, however, and he left college soon after starting.

In 1941, the US entered World War II. The government knew how famous Jesse still was and asked him to help promote fitness to

African Americans as a way to help the war effort. Jesse also worked at a Ford Motors factory in Detroit, Michigan, supervising the hiring of black workers, and was paid to give speeches around the country. He was becoming almost as good a public speaker as he had been a runner! After the war, Jesse left Ford and made money giving more speeches and doing some exhibition running.

In 1949, Jesse moved his family to Chicago, Illinois. At first he worked for a large men's

WORLD WAR II

World War II began with war in Europe, when Nazi Germany invaded Poland. Many countries, including the US, Australia, and Canada, joined forces to battle the Nazis and their allies. The war lasted from 1939 to 1945 and was fought in Europe, Asia, and Africa. Millions of people died on both sides.

Jesse holds a painting created in his honour after he was named "Athlete of the Half-Century" in 1950.

clothing company, but later he had other jobs, including managing an apartment building, helping sell insurance, and holding a position in the Illinois state government.

However, people had not forgotten Jesse's thrilling achievements during the 1936 Olympics. In 1950, Jesse was named "Athlete of the Half-Century" by the Associated Press. He was honoured at a big event in Chicago, where he was able to see many of his Olympic teammates and friends.

The next year, he was invited to Berlin for a ceremony at the Olympic Stadium. While he was there, a German teenager asked Jesse to sign a photo of Jesse with Luz Long at the 1936 Olympics. Jesse was very surprised when the young man said that he was Long's son, Karl. Jesse was thrilled to be able to tell Karl about his father, though sad to hear the details of Luz's death in the war years before.

Throughout the 1950s, Jesse held job after job, almost all connected to his personal fame. In 1955, the US government sent him to Southeast Asia and India to promote American interests. Having a world-famous celebrity there helped US diplomats meet and greet international leaders.

Another highlight was when Jesse was the official US representative at the 1956 Olympic Games in Melbourne, Australia.

On his 1955 trip to India, Jesse helped local track athletes perfect their form...

...and spoke to students about life in America.

Jesse represented the United States at the 1956 Olympics in Melbourne, Australia.

In 1960, Jesse appeared on a TV show. He didn't know he was going to be on it until the show started, however. The show was called "This Is Your Life". The host would surprise a celebrity, and then lead the audience through the person's life. The highlight was the arrival of guests including friends and family. Jesse was shocked to see former teammates, old friends from Ohio, and even his former coach Charles Riley, who was now 82. It was a memorable and humbling event. Jesse smiled throughout. The next decade would not include as many happy moments.

Life gets **complicated**

The 1960s were a difficult time in America. However, at the start of the decade things seemed to be going well for Jesse.

In 1961, Jesse and Ruth proudly watched Marlene become the second Owens daughter to graduate from Ohio State. She broke a barrier of her own by being named the university's first African-American homecoming queen. That year, Jesse also started an advertising company called Owens-West and Associates. He teamed up with an African American called Ted West, who had worked in newspapers.

What is homecoming?

An annual celebration at many colleges. Events are held to welcome back alumni and honour college heroes.

Together, they made the company a success, mostly by using Jesse's name. Jesse would endorse products and Owens-West would help make adverts aimed at African-American audiences. They created a track-and-field event sponsored by an oil company that would be held annually for decades. Owens-West became the most successful business Jesse ever started.

Jesse found time to have some fun with his favourite activity. In 1965, he worked with the New York Mets at the baseball team's spring training. He coached the Mets in running, hoping he could help them steal more bases. Jesse found it a joy to be in the Florida sun, running around with active young athletes.

The sunny days dimmed later that year. Jesse's problems with money continued. The US government charged him, again, for not paying taxes. They said he had not filed any tax returns from 1959 to 1962. He was charged with a crime and taken to court. He could even have been sent to jail. In the end, he had to pay a large fine as well as the taxes owed. Once again, Jesse had to worry about money. He also had to worry about his public image.

The 1960s saw big changes in the United States. African Americans had finally become tired of the many years of discrimination and racism. They were speaking up, marching, and protesting against the laws and situations that held them down. In cities in the South, African Americans organized boycotts of bus lines that made black people sit at the back. They held

African-American students take part in a sit-in at a Woolworth department store in Greensboro, North Carolina.

"sit-ins" at lunch counters that would not serve black customers. They organized events to get more African Americans registered to vote.

Their leaders usually called for non-violent resistance, and Dr Martin Luther King Jr was the most important voice. He called for all people, black and white, to be judged "not by the colour of their skin, but by the content of their character". Still, his followers were loud and vocal. One event he led in 1963 drew more than 250,000 people to Washington, D.C.

MARTIN LUTHER KING

Born in 1929, King trained as a minister, like his father. Angered by discrimination in his home state of Alabama, he became a national leader of the Civil Rights Movement. He gave brilliant and passionate speeches to encourage non-violent resistance even as he called for massive change. King was killed by an assassin in 1968. Martin Luther King Day is celebrated each January in his honour.

At the March on Washington in 1963, Dr King made his famous "I Have a Dream" speech.

Jesse, meanwhile, tried to stay out of this fight. He had spent years working with white people, and wasn't sure now was the time to speak out against them. He was aware of inequality, but felt that the way forward was to be yourself and that change would come eventually.

Things got worse in 1968. King was killed by a gunman in Memphis. Angry riots broke out in many cities. A new kind of protest arose, one that called for violence in response to police violence. Groups such as the Black Panthers called for armed revolution. Jesse did not want this to happen, either.

For Jesse, things came to a head at a familiar place: the Olympic track stadium. At the 1968 Games in Mexico City, American athletes Tommie Smith and John Carlos won medals in the 200 metres. On the medal stand, they appeared wearing black socks and no shoes.

Who were the Black Panthers?

Founded in 1966, they were a political party that called for an end to discrimination. They were later involved in some violent acts.

They held up black-gloved fists as the National Anthem played. It was a hugely visible protest against racism in the United States. Jesse couldn't believe it. He thought that Smith and Carlos, and the many people who agreed with them about what must be done to stop racism, were making a mistake. Then, Jesse made a mistake of his own.

He wrote a book in 1970 called *Blackthink: My life as a Black Man and a White Man*. In the book, Jesse put forward his views on the racial crisis in the US. He said that Smith and Carlos did not speak for "the silent black majority" that he believed simply wanted to work hard to get ahead, as he had. He wrote that the reason that African Americans did not succeed was because they chose to fail.

Jesse's long distance from the racism of his past

Tommie Smith (*centre*) and John Carlos hold up black-gloved fists after winning gold and bronze.

While in the Ivory Coast, Jesse led running clinics to help athletes improve their performance.

blinded him to what was happening. Certainly, he had "made it", but he didn't stop long enough to realize that not every African American could trade on four gold medals to make it in a white person's world.

Jesse's book was harshly criticized by black readers. White newspapers, though, found it refreshing and positive.

Jesse signed up to represent several large corporations. President Richard Nixon even sent Jesse on a goodwill trip to the Ivory Coast, West Africa. That country named a street in its capital in Jesse's honour.

Jesse with Richard Nixon in 1958.

Back in the United States, there were quite
a few African-American neighbourhoods
that would not have done the same.

12

Recovery and **legacy**

By 1972, Jesse had thought hard, and realized that he had to try again, or risk tarnishing his golden legacy.

Jesse wrote another book, this one called *I Have Changed*. In it he explained that he had, indeed, changed his mind. He now recognized that there was still a long way to go until racism was gone in the United States. He pointed out more clearly the many ways in which black people had a hard life. While he still disagreed with violent protest, he wrote that those people did have the right to protest, and that they should. Jesse came to realize that while he had risen to great heights thanks to

By the 1970s, Jesse was a beloved elder statesman of American sport.

the fame he had earned in Berlin, other African Americans were not as lucky.

For most of his life he had believed that his success depended on white people supporting him.

It was difficult for him to let go of this understanding of how the world worked – that black people needed the approval of white people to succeed. With his new book, he made clear that he now understood the full extent of racism against African Americans.

The book helped open the door to the final chapter of his life, when he once again reached national legend status.

Jesse and Ruth moved to Arizona not long after his second book came out – no more cold Chicago winters for them. While living there, Jesse travelled to receive a parade of honours. In 1972, he was given an honorary degree from Ohio State. Jesse had never actually graduated, but the university remembered his actions and his time there fondly.

Jesse receiving his honorary degree from Ohio State.

In 1973, Jesse joined the board of directors of the United States Olympic Committee. The next year, he was elected to the World Track and Field Hall of Fame and got a lifetime achievement award from the NCAA.

President Gerald Ford

Perhaps his biggest honour came in 1976. President Gerald Ford presented Jesse with the Presidential Medal of Freedom. It's the highest award an American civilian can receive, given to people who have made an important contribution to the United States, world peace, or culture.

Sadly, Jesse was diagnosed with lung cancer in 1979. Though an athlete, he had smoked for many years. His race in life finally ended on 31 March 1980.

What is a civilian?

A civilian is a citizen of a country who is not a member of the military.

CARL LEWIS

Like Jesse, Carl Lewis was born in Alabama. However, Carl grew up in New Jersey. He set national high-school records and became the second athlete ever to win college national titles in the 100 metres and long jump. The first? Jesse, of course. Carl reached his first Olympics in 1984 and matched Jesse's total of four golds. He returned to the Games in 1988, 1992, and 1996, ending his amazing career with nine golds and a silver. He is the only athlete to win the long jump at four Olympics in a row.

Four years later, Carl Lewis brought Jesse's memory back into the spotlight. At the Los Angeles Olympics, Lewis won the 100-metre and 200-metre races. He won the long jump and he was part of the gold-medal-winning 4x100-metre relay. Finally, 48 years after Jesse's Berlin achievements, someone had matched him.

All of Jesse's Olympic and world records have now been broken. However, Jesse's name

"I was a **little kid,** I was a late bloomer and **Jesse** said 'You're a little kid, but you can **beat** the **big guys** if you **work hard.'** It was a simple message but **effective."**

Carl Lewis about Jesse Owens

will always be near the top of the greatest Olympic athletes of all time. His gold-medal days in the face of Nazi racism make him an enduring symbol of the battle that must always be fought against such evil. In four thrilling events, Jesse Owens ran that evil into the ground.

Jesse's
family tree

Father

Henry Owens
1881–1942

Emma Owens
1876–1940

Mother

Three older sisters
and six older brothers:
Lillie, Josephine, Ida,
Ernest, Henry, Prentiss,
Johnson, Quincy,
and Sylvester

James Cleveland
"Jesse" Owens
1913–1980

Wife

Ruth Solomon
Owens

1915–2001

Gloria Owens
Hemphill

1932–

Daughter

Marlene Owens
Rankin

1939–

Daughter

Beverly Owens
Prather

1940–

Daughter

Timeline

Jesse Owens is born in Oakville, Alabama, USA, on 12 September.

In eighth grade, Jesse sets his first records for his age group, in long jump and high jump.

1913   c.1922   1928   1932

The Owens family moves to Cleveland, Ohio.

Jesse meets Olympic champion Charles Paddock, inspiring a new goal – to be an Olympic champion himself.

Jesse becomes a dad when his first daughter is born.

USA

Cleveland

Oakville

Jesse begins college at
Ohio State University.

At the Olympics in Berlin,
Germany, Jesse wins gold
medals in four events.

In less than one hour
at the Big Ten finals,
Jesse ties a world
record and sets the
world record for
three other events.

Jesse is suspended
from all AAU
events, ending
his athletic career.

| 1933 | 1935 | 1936 | 1941 |

Jesse and Ruth
get married.

The Associated
Press names Jesse
"Athlete of the Year".

The US enters World War II.
Jesse helps the war effort by
promoting fitness.

Jesse and his family
move to Chicago, Illinois,
where Jesse works in
a wide range of jobs.

Dr Martin Luther
King Jr is assassinated,
sparking more violent
civil-rights protests.

At the Olympic Games
in Melbourne, Australia,
Jesse is the official
US representative.

1949   1950   1951   1956   1961   1968

The Associated Press
names Jesse "Athlete
of the Half-Century".

Jesse returns to Germany
for a ceremony at the
Olympic Stadium in Berlin.

African-American
medalists in track at
the Olympics make
a visible protest
against racism on
the medal stand.

Jesse's daughter
Marlene graduates
at Ohio State
University.

Jesse publishes another book, called
I Have Changed, with a new stance.

Jesse publishes
a book called
Blackthink that
is harshly
criticized by
black readers.

Jesse is awarded
the Presidential
Medal of Freedom.

1970

1972

1974

1976

1980

Jesse receives an
honorary degree from
Ohio State University.

Jesse dies, after
being diagnosed
with lung cancer
the year before.

Jesse is elected to the World
Track and Field Hall of Fame
and gets a lifetime achievement
award from the NCAA.

Quiz

1. What did Jesse's family usually eat for dinner when he was growing up?

2. What track event did Jesse set a national junior-high record in?

3. What position did Jesse's classmates elect him to in high school?

4. How many world records did Jesse tie or break in one hour on "the greatest single-day performance in athletic history"?

5. How did the American Olympic team travel to Germany in 1936?

6. Which was the first Olympic event that Jesse won, setting a new world record?

7. Who raised Jesse's hand to the crowd after he had won the long-jump gold medal?

Did you enjoy the book? Show us what you know!

8 How many gold medals did Jesse win at the 1936 Olympics?

9 What did Jesse find more difficult than he had expected upon returning to the US after the Olympics?

10 What title did the Associated Press give Jesse in 1950?

11 Did Jesse agree with the calls for change that other African Americans were making in the 1960s?

12 What honour did Jesse receive from President Ford?

Answers on page 128

Who's who?

Brundage, Avery
(1887–1975) president
of the International
Olympic Committee
from 1952–1972

Carlos, John
(1945–) bronze medalist in
track at the 1968 Olympics
who made a visible protest
against racism

Cromwell, Dean
(1879–1962) US assistant
track coach at the
1936 Olympics

Draper, Foy
(1911–1943) Jesse's
track teammate at
the 1936 Olympics

Ford, Gerald
(1913–2006) 38th US
president from 1974–1977

Glickman, Marty
(1917–2001) Jesse's
track teammate at
the 1936 Olympics

Hitler, Adolf
(1889–1945) racist and
anti-Semitic dictator of
Nazi Germany, whose
policies started World
War II

Johnson, Cornelius
(1913–1946) African
American who won the
gold medal in the high
jump at the 1936 Olympics

**King Jr, Dr Martin
Luther**
(1929–1968) minister
and national leader
in the Civil Rights
Movement

Lewis, Carl
(1961–) American track-
and-field athlete who
won nine Olympic gold
medals and one silver

Long, Luz
(1913–1943) German long-
jumper at the 1936 Olympics
and friend of Jesse's

Metcalfe, Ralph
(1910–1978) Jesse's track teammate at the 1936 Olympics

Nixon, Richard
(1913–1994) 37th US president from 1969–1974

Owens, Beverly
(1940–) Jesse's youngest daughter

Owens, Emma
(1876–1940) Jesse's mother

Owens, Gloria
(1932–) Jesse's first daughter

Owens, Henry
(1881–1942) Jesse's father

Owens, Marlene
(1939–) Jesse's middle daughter

Paddock, Charles
(1900–1943) American sprinter given the nickname "world's fastest human" in 1921

Riley, Charles
(1878–1960) Jesse's first track coach, starting in junior high

Robertson, Lawson
(1883–1951) US track coach at the 1936 Olympics

Robinson, Bill "Bojangles"
(1878–1949) famous African-American tap dancer, singer, and entertainer, and friend to Jesse

Robinson, Mack
(1914–2000) American sprinter in the 1936 Olympics

Roosevelt, Franklin D.
(1882–1945) 32nd US president from 1933–1945

Smith, Tommie
(1944–) gold medalist in track at the 1968 Olympics, who made a visible protest against racism

Snyder, Larry
(1896–1982) Jesse's track coach at Ohio State University

Solomon, Ruth
(1915–2001) Jesse's wife

Stoller, Sam
(1915–1985) Jesse's track teammate at the 1936 Olympics

Wykoff, Frank C.
(1909–1980) Jesse's track teammate at the 1936 Olympics

Glossary

academic probation
warning that a student's grades are not high enough to stay at college unless they improve. Students often may not compete in sports until their grades improve

amateur
person who plays a sport or pursues an activity for pleasure and not for pay

anti-Semitism
hatred of and discrimination against Jewish people as a group

bankruptcy
state of financial failure caused by not having enough money to pay debts

Big Ten Conference
group of (currently 14) US universities who compete in athletic events against each other

Black Panthers
political party founded in 1966 that called for an end to discrimination against African Americans, which became a militant revolutionary group

boll weevil
insect that eats the cotton plant

boycott
refuse to use, buy, or participate in something as a way of protesting or forcing change

Civil Rights Movement
protest movement against racial segregation, discrimination, and inequality for African Americans in the 1950s and 1960s

Civil War
war between the northern and southern parts of the USA, which lasted from 1861–1865

civilian
citizen of a country who is not a member of the military

criticize
find fault with

dictatorship
government where all the power is held by one leader (the dictator)

discrimination
treating a person or group differently from others in an unfair way

Emancipation Proclamation
document that officially freed all people who were enslaved in the southern United States

foul
violation of the rules of a sport

fraternity
group of students who share the same interests and who often live together

Great Depression
period of low business activity and high unemployment in the 1930s, after a stock market crash where millions of people lost their jobs and life savings

Great Migration
movement after World War I of almost 2 million African Americans from farms in the South to cities in the North

homecoming
annual celebration at many colleges where events are held to welcome back alumni and honour college heroes

hurdles
track event in which runners must leap over barriers

Jim Crow laws
rules that enforced segregation, creating separate public places for white people and black people

laurel wreath
circle made of leaves of the laurel plant that is worn on the head and is a symbol of victory dating back to the Ancient Greeks

Nazi
member of the facist political party controlling Germany from 1933–1945

Olympic Games
international sporting event that takes place every four years

prejudice
unfairly disliking a person or group because of a characteristic such as race or religion

qualifying race
race that narrows the field in a competition: only winners and high finishers advance to the next stage

racism
discrimination or hatred based on a belief that certain races are superior to others by nature

relay

running race in which a series of athletes take turns passing a baton to each other as they each run a section of the race

segregation

separating people by race or class from the rest of society

sharecropping

type of farming in which farmers rented land and paid for it with crops they grew; it worked heavily in favour of the landowners

sportsmanship

fair play, respect for opponents, and winning or losing graciously

tax

money collected by the government from people and businesses for public use

telegram

message sent by a telegraph, which is a system for sending messages by code over connecting wires

World War I

war fought from 1914–1918 between countries mainly in Europe and the Middle East

World War II

war fought from 1939–1945 between countries in nearly every part of the world

Index

Acknowledgements

The author would like to thank: Jesse Owens for living a life filled with so many important moments for us to remember. Thanks also to authors William Baker and Jeremy Schaap for their scholarship on Jesse's life.

DK would like to thank: Polly Goodman for proofreading; Helen Peters for the index; Becky Herrick for compiling the reference section; Victoria Pyke for Anglicization; and Kyair Butts for his insightful and helpful feedback.

ANSWERS TO THE QUIZ ON PAGES 116–117

1. beans and vegetables (meat was a special treat); 2. long jump;
3. student council president (and track team captain); 4. four;
5. by ship; 6. 100 metres; 7. Luz Long; 8. four; 9. making money; 10. Athlete of the Half-Century; 11. no, not at first;
12. the Presidential Medal of Freedom